DECORATIVE ACCESSORIES

MADE FROM

MOULDING

Decorative Accessories made from Moulding

Published by Columba Publishing Company, Inc.
Akron, Ohio USA
Copyright 1998 Columba Publishing Company, Inc.
All rights reserved
First Edition
Manufactured in the United States of America
ISBN 0-938655-60-4

Editors:
    Sheri L. Galat, Esq.
    Carli Kistler Miller

Contributing Framers:
    Carolyn Birchenall, CPF
    Justis Bracken, CPF
    Darren Guerrini
    Bill and Betty Hursey, CPF
    Vivian Kistler, CPF
    Jennifer Kocsis, CPF
    Peter Kolf
    Robert Mayfield, CPF
    Bill Parrie, CPF

Illustrations
    Kelly Ross

Photography
    Heather Protz

10 9 8 7 6 5 4 3 2 1

Please request permission or further information from the Permissions Department, Columba Publishing Company. Inc., 2003 West Market St. Akron, Ohio 44313-6917. USA Telephone: 1.330.836.2619 Fax: 1.330.836.9659

Table of Contents

1. Methods

Designing and Measuring 5
  Architectural Elements 5
  Cutting and Building 6
  Building the Basic Box 7
  Building the Basic Lid 7

2. Materials

Moulding, Tools & Accessories 8
  Hardware 9
  Glazing 9
  Mirrors 9
  Finishing 10
  Lining Interiors 10
  Pricing 10

3. Projects

Section A Basic Frame
  Computer Screen Frame 11
  Bulletin Board 11
  Earring Holder 12
  Harlequin Mirror 12
  Clock with Print 13
  Rustic Clock 13
  Serving or Candle Tray 14
  Floor Screen 15
  Standing or Tabernacle Frame 16
  Mantel Clock 16

Section B The Basic Box
  Collector Box 17
  Tabletop Box 17
  Wall Jewelry Box & Mirror 18
  Colonial Clock 19
  Document or Key Box 20
  Photo Box 20
  Two-Tiered Jewelry Box 21
  Burlwood Box 22
  Business Card Holder 22
  Desk Accessories 23
  Box with Ball Feet 23
  Silver Box 24
  Tissue/Reception Box 25
  Etched Mirror Box 25
  Wall Shelf 26

Section C Advanced Building
  Humidor 27
  Gold Octagon 28
  White Marble Octagon 28
  Octagon Mirror & Shelf 29
  Long Octagon Box 29
  Curio Cabinet with Shelves 30
  Sconces 31

Acknowledgments

Decorative accessories made with moulding have been created by many people in the framing and carpentry industry for as long as moulding has been available. All of the projects in this book are original creations of the framers credited in the text.

Special thanks to Bill Parrie; he is an internationally known trainer in the framing industry, and the builder of nearly half of the projects in this book.

We would also like to acknowledge these creative people and organizations for their contribution to the world of moulding projects:

Cliff Bonnie CPF

Decor Magazine

Leslie Sieswerda, CPF

Larson-Juhl

Roma Moulding

Marguerite Day

Professional Picture Framers Association

Greg Perkins, CPF

Jeff Tichenor, CPF

Thanhardt Burger

This book started in 1996 when framer Carolyn Birchenall brought in the architectural elements (page 5). When I pointed out a shelf made of moulding in a mail order catalogue she went to her car and brought me several shelves (pg 26), accessories she had been building for years. Later that month framer Bill Parrie was visiting our offices and brought me a box (pg 22) as a gift. A week later Peter Kolf sent me the box on page 17. Well . . . things just started to add up—so here we are with 39 projects contributed by nine framers. Mouldings used in the projects were often chosen by the framer because they were scraps and fit the need. You may find that the moulding stated has been discontinued—possibly why it was a scrap. You will no doubt have many scraps to substitute. We all hope you find inspiration to build a few things and even use up some of those scraps.

Vivian Kistler
Editor and Publisher

The following companies and products are mentioned in this book:

Mouldings:
    Arquati Co.
    Robert F. de Castro, Inc.
    Decor Moulding Ltd.
    Guerrini
    LaMarche Moulding and Frame Co.
    Larson-Juhl
    Piedmont Moulding
    Presto Frame & Moulding, Inc.
    Eric Schuster
    Valley Moulding & Frame
    Victor Moulding Co.
    The Williamson Co.
    Zinsel Co.

Other Materials:
    AMS, Art Material Service, Inc.
    Rag Mat and Moorman Fabric Covered Matboards, Crescent Cardboard
    FrameMaster, #5 Point Driver, The Fletcher-Terry Co.
    Bumpons, 924, 811, Scotch/3M
    Bainbridge Fabric Matboard, Neilsen & Bainbridge
    Titebond, Franklin, International
    CornerWeld, FrameMica, Co.
    Lineco, Lineco, Inc.
    Elmer's Glue, Borden
    Ser Strap Clamp, Cornerstone Frame Products
    Sobo
    Silicone, Dow Corning
    Velcro, Velcro, USA
    EaselMate, Albin Products
    X-Acto Knife, Hunt Mfg.

CHAPTER 1
METHODS
DESIGNING & MEASURING

Working only with the projects shown in this book could fill many busy hours and result in a fine assortment of accessories; but trying different mouldings and customizing sizes to suit different needs will require an understanding of the principles involved in designing and measuring for these projects.

Just as the artwork or objects being framed guide decisions when designing picture framing, the function of a moulding accessory will guide its design. When function drives the design, begin with the function, measuring to accommodate the job the finished object will perform, such as sufficient length and depth for neckties to hang, or enough width to hold travel brochures, etc.

If the project being built can be any size desired, begin by selecting the main moulding for the design. Often a moulding will have obvious repeats in its ornamentation, or will have a particular character, such as sleek or opulent, that will help determine decisions about size and proportion. In these cases, begin by cutting a key part of the project from this moulding, then make the rest of the design decisions based on this key part.

The project instructions will sometimes say to "cut to fit" or "measure as you go". Because of the endless possible combinations of mouldings, there will frequently be no better way to create a precision assembly of the project. As the process of measuring and problem-solving throughout the project becomes comfortable, the ability to design more creatively will develop.

A VERY EASY PROJECT—
ARCHITECTURAL ELEMENTS

This is a great way to use scraps of beautiful mouldings, when there isn't enough to make even the smallest picture frame. Hang two or more together for a unique wall accent.

Materials:
  Moulding:
      Arquati #867 810 081
  Strap clamp
  Hanging hardware

1) Cut moulding at a normal 45 degree angle, alternating the cuts until you have four each of the moulding triangles. In the example shown above, the moulding was shifted to make the corner ornamentation match attractively. These decisions will change with each moulding.
2) Glue all four pieces together. Hold until glue becomes tacky, then secure with strap clamp.
3) Attach hangers.

ARCHITECTURAL ELEMENTS

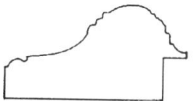

A two foot strip of moulding can be cut in alternating 45 degree angles to create 4 pieces of each cut to join as an element. Smaller mouldings will require less moulding while larger ones will need more length.

CUTTING

Before exploration of the possibilities available in moulding projects can really begin, one must learn to see moulding from different orientations. The instructions in this book will refer to four different perspectives when discussing the building of the projects.

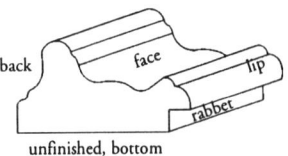

unfinished, bottom

Four Perspectives:

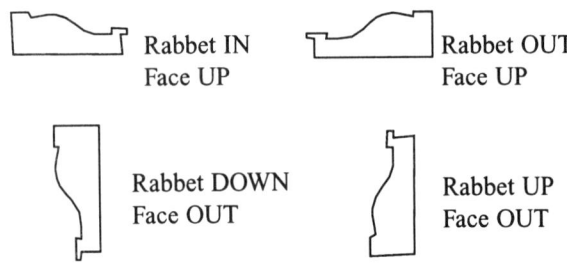

Rabbet IN
Face UP

Rabbet OUT
Face UP

Rabbet DOWN
Face OUT

Rabbet UP
Face OUT

CUTTING

ELECTRIC SAW

A table saw or electric miter box will be the most versatile because any type of moulding can be cut and at most any angle.

CHOPPER

Cutting on the chopper will be restricted because of the issue of supporting moulding pieces with hollows as part of the design on the sides or face of the moulding. The hollows will crush in the chopper.

Each project shows how the moulding will be used. Depending on the type of cutting tool being used, different placements of the moulding may be required. Use the illustrations above to understand the meaning of the terms used in this book, then cut as necessary to yield moulding pieces with the necessary attributes for the project.

DEGREE OF ANGLE REQUIRED FOR PROJECTS INCLUDED IN THIS BOOK:

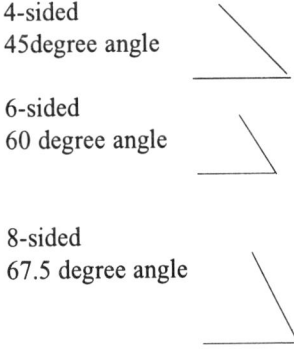

4-sided
45degree angle

6-sided
60 degree angle

8-sided
67.5 degree angle

BUILDING

Assembling moulding maybe tricky because the moulding may not fit into traditional vises. Use strap clamps, c-clamps or jigs that are made from scrap wood, or even mount boards can be utilized to create a support while the frame is drying.

VERY SMALL FRAMES

Sometimes portions of a project will be so small that they will not fit in a vice and cannot be securely gripped with a strap clamp. Glue these pieces together and hold them together with rubber bands, or just glue and hold by hand, adding new pieces as each previous one becomes set.

Try building these on a piece of glass for easy removal, as stray glue can seep from the seams and adhere moulding pieces to the building surface.

BUILDING MULTI-ANGLE FRAMES

Some manufacturers make adapters to join shapes like hexagons and octagons on their joiners. Some standard vises may have adjusting angles to adapt to different angles. Building a jig from wood strips nailed to a plywood board may be necessary.

ASSEMBLING MOULDING LAYERS

For some projects, mouldings can be glued together in advance, then cut as one unit. Be careful to support each layer as the glue dries, keeping rabbets aligned and level.

GLUE

Titebond® or resin carpenter's glue will join most wood mouldings allowing them to be snapped apart after the joins dry. CornerWeld® is a very permanent glue for wood. Once the join is dry a saw will be necessary to open the joint. The combination of glue and nails is the best.

BUILDING A BASIC BOX

- This is the base of many projects.
- Often used "rabbet up", so the width of moulding becomes depth of the box and the rabbet of the moulding becomes a convenient ledge for the lid.
- If the lid or door will be hinged to this box, the box sides or edges will need to be flat enough to securely hold the hinge and allow the door to open easily.

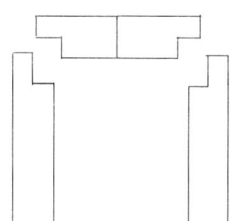

Moulding used as the lid with the rabbet facing outward will provide a lip to set on the edge of the box

This is an example of a moulding cut rabbet up, face out, Moulding: LaMarche #150-3J-010

BUILDING A BASIC LID

- Lids are usually cut and built as ordinary picture frames. For this reason, it is often easier to build the lid first, then build the box to fit the lid size.

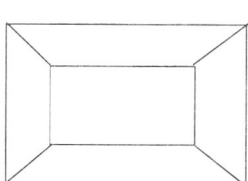

Four pieces of moulding cut at a typical 45 degree angle.

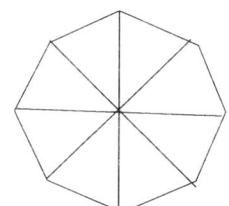

A lid created with 8 pieces of moulding cut at 67.5 degree angle.

45 degree cuts are used to make this rectangular lid.

- Lids are either set onto a ledge, or hinged "door-style" to a flat-sided base.
- The opening in the assembled lid can be filled with additional frames, mirrors, wooden panels, glassed prints or photos, fabric-covered boards, etc. Octagonal lids often have little or no opening where the points come together in the center.

If the lid will have a knob, make sure the lid filler is a material that can securely hold the knob when lifted repeatedly. Cover underside of lid with an attractive surface that coordinates with the overall project. Fabric-covered matboards are suitable.

Two mouldings facing outward to create a lid.

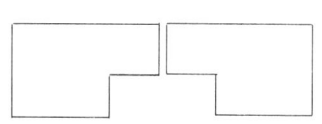

Two mouldings facing inward to create a lid.

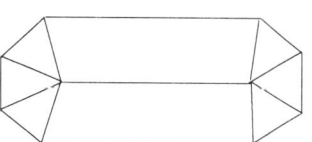

67.5 degree cuts are used to make this octagon lid.

CHAPTER 2

MATERIALS

MOULDING, TOOLS & ACCESSORIES

MOULDING

Picture frame moulding is a wonderful basic material for many projects. With all of the fabulous profiles, sizes, and finishes available, resources are endless. Plus, since many mouldings are introduced as full lines that include a range of sizes from wide and massive to a narrow fillet, beautifully coordinated materials are readily available to the frameshop.

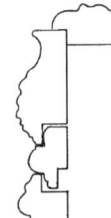

Any moulding can be a source of decorative accessories. Some projects may be created using just one moulding, but many will require stacking and inverting several different ones. Learn to look at mouldings with an eye trained to the project concept. Start testing mouldings next to each other, on top of one another, and inside one another—that's where the fun really begins!

FILLETS

Fillets are available in a huge variety of styles and finishes. This is very fortunate, because fillets are a tremendously valuable tool for these projects. Use fillets to create ledges, to separate layers, to finish edges, and to add a visually attractive polish to many designs.

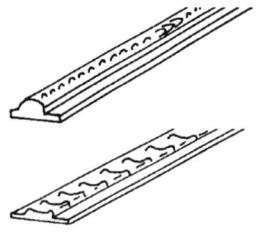

Fillets typically consist of two parts: a recessed back edge (shelf), and a lip (decorative edge). The size of both parts varies tremendously from one fillet to another.

ENHANCERS OR SLIPS

These finished moulding accessories are designed to add to frames for specific purposes; to increase depth, provide a decorative lip, or create finished rabbets inside shadowboxes. For accessory projects, experiment with these used in all sorts of orientations—backwards, sideways, upsidedown.

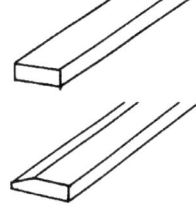

STRETCHER BARS, STRAINER LENGTH, AND RAW LINERS

Raw wood in various forms and sizes will be very helpful for many purposes; bracing, extending, and providing an unfinished surface that can be made to match any look by staining, painting, or finishing.

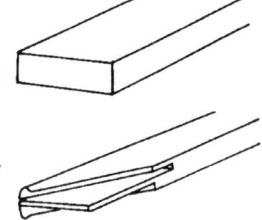

TOOLS & ACCESSORIES

One of the great things about making decorative accessories from moulding is that the tools necessary are typically part of a basic frame workshop. The skills required—cutting moulding, joining it, lining the interior, backing it attractively and attaching hardware—are basically those used in framing.

A general list of the tools and accessories:

Saw and/or chopper (sharp blades are very important)
Goggles when cutting (some of the moulding pieces will be very small, creating small flying bits).
Vise with adjustable angles
Underpinner, may be used in many, but not all projects
Strap Clamp®   Drill   Awl   Hammers
Screwdrivers   Point driver   Nail gun
Staple gun   X-Acto® Knife   Sandpaper
3M924 Double-sided tape, 3M811 Removable tape
Nail-hole filler, putty or other wood filler
Stain, paint, permanent markers
Bumpons®, brass feet, small felt pads
A variety of hardware for feet, handles, knobs

ADHESIVES

Use clean, secure adhesives that have longevity. For wood: CornerWeld®, Titebond®, or carpenters glue. For Fabric: Lineco NpH®, Elmer's®, Tacky®, or Sobo® are suitable for different types of projects. Clear Dow Corning® 100% silicone adhesive can be used to attach a frame to a frame that may have to be separated at a later date.

Do not use rubber cement—it is not a permanent adhesive. Many hot glues are not appropriate because they break in cold temperatures.

FABRIC-COVERED BOARDS

Use the wide variety of beautiful fabric-covered boards available from the matboard manufacturers for the lining, backing, and bottom surfaces of projects. Suedes, moires, and linens work well. The imitation suede-covered matboards are especially easy to use, because they have no nap or grain and do not fray. If the white core of matboards does not suit the design, try cutting reverse bevels, or use black core versions of the boards, or color the exposed core with paint or permanent markers. Several "suede" boards are available in black core as well as other colors.

Fabric must be permanently mounted to matboards using heat/dry mounting, wet glues or pressure-sensitive adhesives.

BACKING MATERIALS

The unseen filler and backing boards fill gaps, increase strength and rigidity, and provide a smooth surface for attachment of a decorative bottom to boxes.

CLAMPS

The Ser Strap Clamp® is a combination of clamps and a flexible strap which provides strong, equal pressure surrounding surfaces, holding them securely while glue dries. This is an indispensable aid in joining multi-angle frames and in numerous other projects.

C-clamps, table clamps, bench vises, paper clamps, and even rubber bands may be helpful when holding small sections together while glue dries.

HARDWARE

Most hardware items may be purchased from typical sources, but try hobby and craft stores for special decorative hardware like feet, handles, and small hinges. Keep in mind the hardness and depth of the moulding, and the weight of the finished project, when selecting hardware. Also be aware of the angle at which screws will be attached, and make sure that the screws required for the hardware are not too long for the moulding.

HANGERS

Strap or mirror hangers, sawtooth hangers, keyhole and D-rings, shelf hangers, recessed hangers, and other carpentry hanging hardware may also be needed. WallBuddies® are flat, triangle brackets that attach to the outside top edge of frames. These are very strong and act as braces on work under stress.

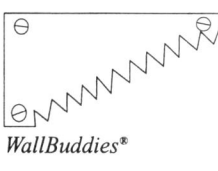
WallBuddies®

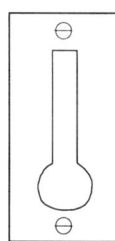
D-rings or
strap hangers

keyhole hanger

HINGES, HANDLES & KNOBS

Most often available from hardware stores, the size, number and placement will vary with each project. Hinges are usually available in chrome or brass finish, and occasionally in black, but can be painted to suit the project.

Some cabinet handles and knobs can be adapted for use in these projects. Finials from lamp departments will make stunning box knobs. They have visual impact and help establish the character of the finished products they decorate.

Be on the lookout for interesting objects that can be knobs, not only at hardware and decorating stores, but at flea markets and antique stores also. Embossed small brass doorknobs and old lamp finials can make great knobs. Craft stores offer a good selection of small hinges. Brass, black and chrome hinges and findings are available in the framing industry from Art Materials, Inc. (AMS).

EASEL BACKS

The Albin EaselMate® is a small stand made in a simple "T" shape. It is attached to the bottom edge of the frame and allows the most support with minimal infringement on the design project.

GLAZING

TYPES

Several projects in this book use glass or mirror. Look into specialty framing glass. Anti-reflective, Museum glass and ultraviolet filtering glazing may be suitable for your projects.

FITTING GLAZING

Often glass will be viewed from both sides so the method to hold it in the box will need to be "invisible". Some suggestions follow:

• Glazier's points are available from Fletcher for both the FrameMaster® and the #5 Point Driver. Glazier's points are 3/8" while framer's points are 5/8". Once driven into the moulding they are not visible from the front of the frame. If the points will be seen from the back side of the project a cover can be made from fillet or strips of suede matboard.

• Silicone, clear, neutral cure Dow Corning 794 or 796, may be used to secure frames, glazing or to seal-off the rabbet of a glass tray. However, silicone must cure before sealing into a frame project. Use the smallest amount possible. Silicone may tarnish some metals and adversely affect items that are calcium-carbonate based such as seashells.

MIRRORS

Mirrors can be placed in any custom frame that can handle the weight of the mirror itself (which can get quite heavy in larger sizes.) Mirrors offer a terrific opportunity for experimenting with multi-angle frames, including octagons, elongated hexagons, etc.

Paint the inside of the rabbet black or the color of the frame, because the mirror will reflect the under edge of the moulding lip; if it is unfinished or the finish is irregular the edge will reflect into the mirror and be visible to the viewer.

Note—Use high quality 1/8" mirror for small frames, to minimize weight, and 1/4" mirror for larger frames, for viewing clarity.

FINISHING

LINING INTERIORS

Boxes, cabinets and cases need to be neatly lined. Fabric-covered matboard is easy to use for these projects. Measure carefully, then experiment with templates of board of the thickness chosen for the lining before cutting the actual pieces. Remember to compensate for board thickness, as precision size and well-matched seams are a key part of a well-made moulding accessory. Don't force the fit—matboard under pressure will eventually buckle.

LIDS

Make lids fit securely and make inner walls flush with frame edges by choosing boards of suitable thicknesses. Attach lining pieces to moulding with glue or 3M#924 tape. In some projects, lining pieces can be attached to the moulding before moulding is joined.

UNDER SIDES AND BACK SIDES

Use glue, 3M#924 tape, or nails to attach fabric-covered board pieces or other base materials to the bottom surfaces of the projects. If using nails, be sure to slightly countersink them or the scratchy nailheads will defeat the purpose of the soft fabric surface!

Make bottom surface covers slightly smaller than the actual dimensions of the bottom, for an attractive finished look that will fit neatly and won't compete visually with the bottom edges of the moulding. If edges of matboard must be painted, do so before attaching it to the base.

In some cases, Bumpons® may be needed on the bottom of the design, to prevent it from slipping around. For example, a lightweight box with a moiré board base may be fine sitting on a mantel, but may constantly slide out of place on an entryway table. Adhesive-backed felt pads or Bumpons® are useful for items that will usually sit still. Decorative feet or tacks may be necessary for items that need to be moved frequently.

FINISHING

Be certain all nail holes and joins are filled. Sand and touch up rough edges. Glue stray fabric threads. Use a critical eye but be realistic. Variation and individuality are characteristics of even the finest quality hand-crafted items. This bit of extra attention will give these moulding projects the same professional character that sets the standard of fine custom framing.

HINGES

Sometimes the area where a hinge will be placed will need to be routed out, so that the hinge will be recessed, flush with the edge of the moulding. If this is needed, use the hinge as a template and trace the proper placement on the moulding. Clamp the moulding in place if necessary to hold it stable, then cut out the penciled area to the depth of the hinge. An X-Acto® Knife is usually strong enough to cut away the wood.

OTHER HARDWARE

Clasps, knobs, and handles should be securely screwed or nailed in place. Test before and after attachment to make sure that functional hardware actually works, drawers open, doors meet flush, etc.

PRICING

Once a moulding project is successfully completed, how does one determine a suitable price for these unique works of art?

One guideline is *market value*. Look for similar items in stores and catalogues to determine typical prices.

Another consideration is the cost of time and materials. This should not be based on the effort and supplies required for a first attempt—some investment in the learning process must be expected—but after a few projects a general standard of cost can be established.

If the product price based on investment far exceeds the market value, an adjustment will have to be made—cheaper materials, speedier methods, lower profit margin, or building them just for fun.

CHAPTER 3

PROJECTS
SECTION A   THE BASIC FRAME

COMPUTER SCREEN FRAME
BY VIVIAN KISTLER

This is a fun and easy first project, since it is really just an ordinary picture frame used in a new way. It is perfect for any frame shop that is using computers. Flat-style profiles are appropriate and attach securely to the monitor.

Materials:
Moulding:
  Williamson #38-6465-4340
Adhesive-backed Velcro®, circles or strips.

1) Measure the computer monitor. Make sure the "on" light and any other buttons will remain visible and available.
2) Select a moulding that has a flat back and does not protrude beyond the monitor case. If the back side is visible when mounted to the monitor, cover the back of the moulding with fabric-covered board.

Computer screen frames must allow the controls to be seen and accessed.

BULLETIN BOARD
BY VIVIAN KISTLER

Bulletin boards can be made from any moulding. Sleek and modern, elegant and ornate, rustic natural. Bulletin boards can also be attached to refrigerators with magnetic strips available at craft stores.

Materials:
Moulding:
  DeCastro #11966
Foam center board, 3/16"
Mounting adhesive
Fabric, ribbons or cords are optional

1) Mount fabric to a piece of foam center board, using wet, dry mounting or cold mount films.
2) Wrap cording around corners diagonally or criss-crossed. Use a straight pin to secure the ends into the edge of the foam center board. These cords create "pockcts" for inscrting itcms that should not be pierced with pins.
3) Fill the rabbet with another piece of foam board or scrap matboards to provide support for the pushing of pins. Fit as usual.

Bulletin boards can be made from any size frame using covered foam center board.

Hardware options are on page 9.

EARRING HOLDER

BY VIVIAN KISTLER

This easel-backed frame holds wire earrings. It can also be made without the easel back, to hang on the wall.
To accommodate post-style earrings, don't use any backing board or easelback; attach an Albin EaselMate® to the bottom edge of the frame (page 9).

Materials:
    Moulding:
        Eric Schuster #57-38-0023
          and scrap narrow black moulding
    Matboard: Crescent #SRM4420
    Silver, brass or black wire mesh (craft or hardware store)
    Hanging hardware or easel back
To hold the mesh in place:
1) Build a strainer to fit the rabbet of the frame, using any narrow moulding; leave sufficient allowance for mesh to wrap around sides.
2) Stretch wire mesh over strainer and staple in place.
3) Set into the rabbet.
4) Set a decorative matboard over the stretched wire and fit into the frame.

Hardware options are on the page 9.

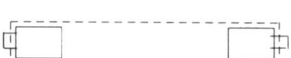

Wrap mesh around a strainer or frame made from small scrap moulding. Staple the mesh into the sides of the strainer.

HARLEQUIN MIRROR

BY CAROLYN BIRCHENALL

Materials:
    Moulding:
        Artisan Moulding #12096
    Mirror, wood balls
    Paint, glue, 3M#811 removable tape, brads

1) The harlequin design is added to the moulding by masking off the shape with removable tape and painting the sections.
2) Nail brads into the wooden balls leaving 1/2" of nail exposed. Poke into a styrofoam block to make painting all sides of the balls easier.
3) Mark placement of balls on edge of frame. Drill holes into frame, apply glue to nails and insert the nail with the ball attached into the holes. Wooden balls may also be attached directly to the frame with CornerWeld®, a permanent wood glue.
4) Paint the rabbet black before inserting mirror.

Hardware options are on page 9.

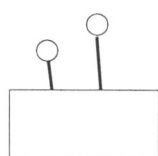

Stick wooden balls into a block of Styrofoam for ease of painting.

CLOCK WITH PRINT

BY CAROLYN BIRCHENALL

Materials
    Moulding:
        Larson-Juhl #404N
    Matboards:
        Crescent #48406 Grecian Gold
        Crescent #1576 Dark Gray
    Clock movement & face
    Foam center board
    Small engraving

1) Build frame, 11-1/4x16" rabbet size.
2) Trim #48406 to 11-1/4x16". Cut a V-groove 2" from outside edge. Cut a circle mat in the upper area of the mat, about 1/2" larger than the clock face. Cut a window mat in lower half of board along V-groove.
3) Cut a 1-1/2" mat of foam center board. Install glass, mat, and foam center mat in frame.
4) Cut a double mat with a circle opening for the clock face and a rectangle opening for the small print.
5) Attach print to mat. Attach a backing board behind print. Install clock face in mat. Support clock works with pieces of foam center board as needed.
6) Cover back. Cut an opening in backing to expose battery compartment of clock works. Attach hangers to frame.

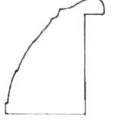
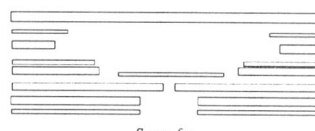

glass
gold mat
foam center board
double mat, clock
gold mat
foam center bd.
gold backing

*Space for
battery*

RUSTIC CLOCK

BY VIVIAN KISTLER

This is simply an interesting moulding used as a clock.
Materials:
    Moulding:
        De Castro, Rafters #8002
    Matboard:
        Crescent Moorman #7553
    Clock movement and numerals
    Foam center board

1) Build the frame. Cut a linen matboard 7" square.
2) Punch a hole in the center for the clock movement, attach the numerals with CornerWeld®. Fit the linen board into the frame.
3) On the back side, support the clock battery with pieces of foam center board. Cut a piece of linen matboard to cover the entire back side of the clock, leaving an opening for access to the clock battery and dials.

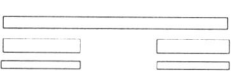

linen board
foam center bd.
linen back board

*Space for
battery*

SERVING OR CANDLE TRAY

BY BILL PARRIE

Trays can be made in many sizes. For easy balance when carrying, proportions should be approximately those of standard picture frames: 12 x 16", 16 x 20" or a little more rectangular such as 14 x 20".

Although very large, very long and narrow, or exactly square trays can be difficult to handle as serving trays, they are stunning as candle trays or for table centerpieces.

Be creative with the face of the tray visible beneath the glass surface. Use fabric-covered matboard, mounted reproductions, decorative paper, or fabrics. Make a collage of antique postcards or holiday cards. Make trays featuring a multi-opening mat with family photographs. For a more formal look, use mirror as the tray surface instead of ordinary glass.

Materials:
  Moulding:
    Larson-Juhl #347VBG for tray
    Larson-Juhl #145BL for handles
  Glass or mirror
  Silicone Adhesive
  Fabric-covered panel to place under glass
  Two handles, purchased or made from moulding
  Bainbridge #4165
  Bumpons or ball feet

1) Cut and join moulding as an ordinary frame. Shallow, flat mouldings are most appropriate. Paint rabbet black if using mirror as tray face.
2) Run a very thin, continuous band of silicone all the way around the inside of the rabbet. Set the glass in place on the silicone bead*. This will prevent liquid spills on the tray from seeping into the boards beneath the glass. Acrylic sheeting may be used instead of glass for lighter weight, but the acrylic surface is easily scratched.
3) Fit fabric-covered board into frame.
4) Fill the frame rabbet with matboard or a combination of matboard and foam center board.
5) Attach suede matboard to back of tray. Use adhesive instead of nails so that back is smooth and will not scratch surfaces. Attach bumpons or brass feet.
6) Attach handles to sides of tray. The handles shown are made by attaching a 2-1/2" strip of moulding to the center of each short side with glue and nails, then attaching a 1-1/2"strip of the same moulding to the first strips.

* See silicone information on page 9.

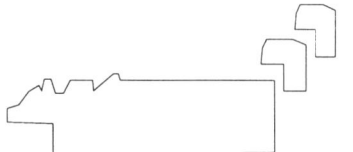

Tray handle is made from 2 pieces of small black moulding cut one smaller than the other and glued and nailed together. Handles must be secure.

THREE-PANEL FLOOR SCREEN
BY BILL PARRIE

Depending on the size, these directions can be used to make a fireplace screen, room divider, or small tabletop decoration. Use a moulding with a flat outside edge, so that the screen will sit securely on a surface. Also make sure the moulding looks attractive when two pieces of it are placed back to back.

Combinations of moulding and screen faces, can result in a wide variety of styles from an elegant, formal furniture piece, to a playful-looking divider for a child's room. The screen face can be fabric, wallpaper, painted or faux-finished matboard, etc.

Materials:
Moulding:
Larson-Juhl #349WB
Fabric-covered matboard
Filler board
Two sets (pairs) of double-action hinges

1) Build six frames. Sizes must be precise, to have the frames line up when positioned back-to-back.
2) Attach fabric-covered panels into all six frames.
3) To create one panel:
   • Lay one frame (with panel inserted) face down.
   • Add a layer of filler board such as foam center board behind each panel to fill rabbet.
   • place a frame face up on the stack.
4) Attach the frames together, creating three sets. If wood glue is used, the connection will be permanent. If preferred, frames can be attached to one another with dab of silicone adhesive*, which can be sliced with a razor blade and separated if the panels ever require repairs or replacement.
5) Attach hinges to connect frames. If the frame panels are very large, add a third hinge centered between the first two, or use a single piano hinge the length of the project, for stability.

* See page 9 for more information about silicone.

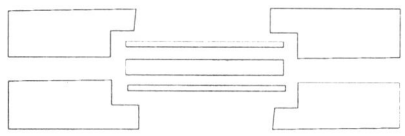

Plan rabbet depth to accommodate a sheet of foam center board and two pieces of fabric covered matboard.

Instead of fabric panels, cut mats from fabric-covered matboards such as linen or suede. Sheets of Mylar can be used as a face-covering for the photos or artwork.*

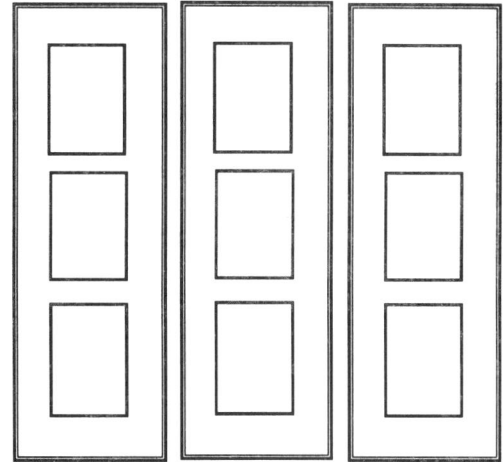

STANDING FRAME

BY BILL PARRIE

Materials:
  Moulding:
    Larson-Juhl #305GB
  Matboard: Crescent Moorman #7195
  Glass, Turn buttons

1) Cut and join a picture frame for a 4 x 6 photo.
2) Bevel the edges of suede board to fit the back of the frame.
3) Cut 5/8" mat using the bevel-edged backing board. Save the fallout. Glue mat to back of frame.
4) Lay fallout in center of mat and hold in place using turnbuttons, two on each long side of the frame.
5) To make base, use #305GB, rabbet up, face out, sized to fit the bottom rail of the photo frame.
6) Attach frame to base using glue and nails from the bottom.
7) Finish bottom of frame with piece of suede board matching backing board.
8) Fit glass in frame opening using glazier's points.

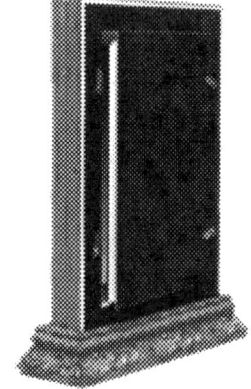
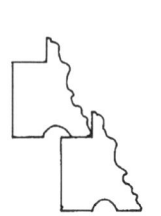

THE MANTEL CLOCK

BY JUSTIS BRACKEN

Materials:
  Moulding:
    Valley Moulding #67745 Gold, clock face
    Valley Moulding #63775-BK, base
  Matboard: Crescent #61038
  Clock works

1) Cut and join clock frame 5 x 5" rabbet size.
2) Create clock face: Cut a 5 x 5" square of matboard. V-groove a horizontal and vertical center line, to indicate numerals 3, 6, 9, and 12. Make a hole in center for clock hands.
3) Cut a 2-1/2" beveled circle of matboard. Make a hole in the center for clock hands. Glue circle in center.
4) Fit clock face into face frame.
5) Cut a mat to cover back of clock frame, with beveled opening for battery-powered clockworks.
6) Build base: cut a three-sided frame, one front piece with a 7-1/2" rabbet measure, and two side pieces with a 1" rabbet measure (2" outside). Join.
7) Paint back of base frame black.
8) Attach clock to base from the bottom with screws.
9) Attach hands and clock works to clock face.

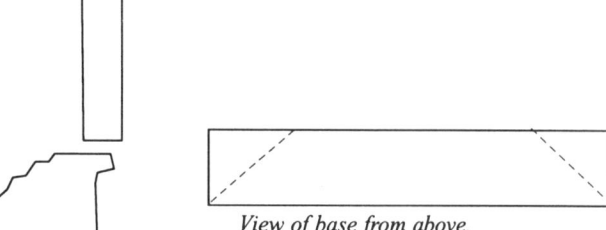

View of base from above.

COLLECTOR BOX

BY DARREN GUERRINI

With clear glass in its lid, this makes a great coffee table display box for a special item or small group of items. Line the box with a dark color to show off white or light objects, or with light colors for dark objects.

    Materials:

        Moulding:

            Guerrini #225 5146

        Matboard: Crescent Moorman #67114

        One piece regular or "invisible" glass

        Foam center board

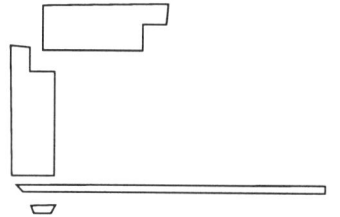

1) Cut and build a normal picture frame for the lid.
2) Cut a suede board mat to cover the underside of the lid. Bevel outside edge and attach.
3) Fit glass with glazier's points. Cover exposed points with narrow strips of suede board or fillet.
4) Cut base frame, rabbet up, face out, to fit lid. Join frame.
5) Paint the rabbet inside the box or cut a suede board mat to cover it.
6) Line sides of box interior with suede board. Make board pieces end just short of bottom edge, then cut a piece of suede board to fit inside bottom of box, facing inward. Lay the box face down. Set the bottom lining in place, suede facing the box interior. Use point driver to secure board in place.
7) Cut a piece of suede board, with beveled edges, to cover the bottom of the box. Attach with glue or double sided tape.

TABLETOP BOX

BY PETER KOLF

    Materials:

        Moulding:

            Presto #425, base

            Presto #013, lid

        Matboard: Crescent Moorman #67106

        Glass, Print

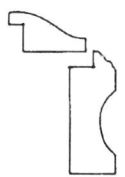

1) Build lid frame to fit print.
2) Fit glass and print into lid.
3) Cover inside of lid with matboard.
4) Build base to fit lid.
5) Line box with matboard.
6) Cover bottom of box with matboard.

WALL JEWELRY BOX & MIRROR

BY BILL PARRIE

Mirrors can be functional as well as decorative. This wall hanging mirror is mounted in a hinged door to allow a shallow compartment box behind it.

Materials:
Moulding:
Larson-Juhl #373IG, front and shelf
Larson-Juhl #643IG, box
Matboard: Bainbridge #4839
Mirror, size 14 x 50"
Hinges, cup hooks or other decorative hangers

1) Build frame to fit mirror. Fit mirror in frame. Cover back of frame with matboard.
2) Create box rabbet down, face out.
3) Line interior with matboard. Fit matboard and foam center board into rabbet at back of box.
4) Make shelf pieces rabbet up, face out, one strip for front of shelf and two short pieces for sides. Fit matboard and foam center board in shelf.
5) Attach hooks to shelf. Hinge door to box. Attach magnet or clasp closure if desired. Attach hanging hardware, see options on page 9.

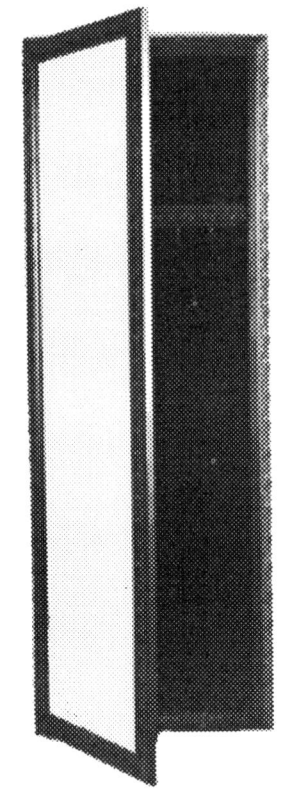
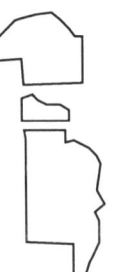

WALL CLOCK WITH SECRET COMPARTMENT

BY BILL PARRIE

Materials:
Moulding:
Larson-Juhl #347VMG, face
Larson-Juhl #157VG, fillet for trim
Larson-Juhl #X2362, box
Matboard: Crescent Moorman #7199
Clock face and works
Hinges

1) Cut and join face frame: 13-1/4" square rabbet size.
2) Cut box moulding rabbet up face out.
3) Trim edge of box with the fillet.
4) Line interior with suede matboard.
5) Attach clock face and works.
6) Hinge face frame to box frame.
7) Attach hanging hardware to back. Use D-rings or "keyhole" hangers, routing out hardware area so clock will hang flush.

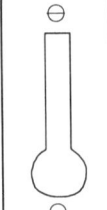

COLONIAL CLOCK

BY PETER KOLF

Clocks are a great practical moulding project. Clocks are made like other boxes, with the clock face portion fitted into a hinged "lid". The hands and face and the internal mechanical "works" can be found in a variety of styles at craft stores and through mail order clock-making suppliers.

The moulding for the front of this clock is a reproduction of an Empire moulding commonly used in the 1800s and frequently seen on clocks in antique shops. The lower portion of the front is glassed to display the swinging brass pendulum.

Materials:
> Moulding:
>> Presto #076, face frame
>> Presto #070T, dividing strip on clock face
>> Presto #425, extender for base
> Matboard for interior, face: Crescent Moorman #7540
> Clock face and works
> Glass, Hardware: two hinges and one clasp

1) Cut and join frame for front of clock 9-1/2 x 21" rabbet size.
2) Determine size of clock face, then attach dividing strip to rabbet of frame where face will end.
3) Set glass above and below dividing strip using glazing points. (see page 9).
4) Build extender frame, rabbet will face the back wall. Cover extender frame, including back, with matboard.
5) Cut a circle mat from same color board to fit clock face.
6) Install clockworks and matted clock face into upper portion of the face frame.
7) Hinge face frame to extender frame on left side. Attach clasp on right side.
8) Clock can stand on shelf or mantel or attach hanging hardware to hang clock on wall.

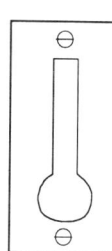

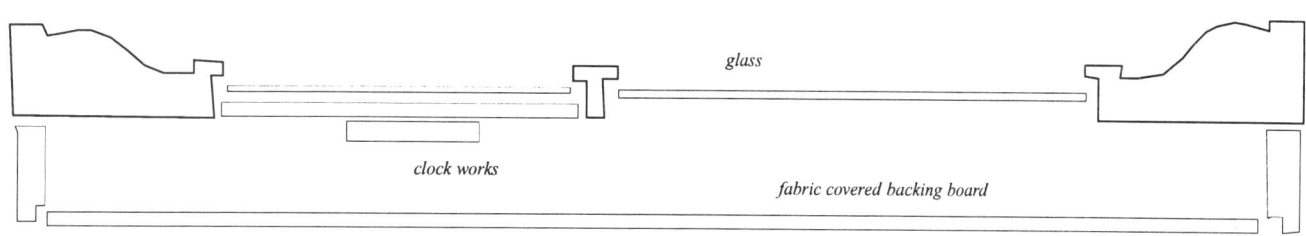

glass

clock works

fabric covered backing board

DOCUMENT OR KEY BOX

BY BILL PARRIE

Materials:
    Moulding:
        Larson-Juhl #419721, lid
        Larson-Juhl #619721, base of box
    Matboard: Crescent Moorman #7195
    Double-matted print for lid
    Hinges

This box is designed to hang on the wall, with a compartment behind the print. The space inside would be perfect for mounting hooks to hold keys. In this design, the base is cut about 1" smaller all the way around than the lid, creating an interesting shape.

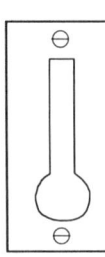

PHOTO BOX

BY BILL PARRIE

This is a great way to keep a selection of photographs handy but unobtrusive. Make the depth to accommodate as many photos as desired.

Materials:
    Moulding
        Larson-Juhl #357VS, lid
        Larson-Juhl #727VS, box
    Matboard: Crescent #A7201
    Hinges
    Print or Matted photo to fit lid
    Glass to fit lid

1) Cut and join lid. Fit a matted photo in frame opening. Cover underside of lid with fabric covered matboard.
2) Cut box, rabbet up face out. Join and line box.
3) Hinge lid to box.
4) Cover bottom with fabric matboard.

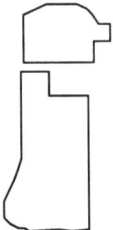

Two-Tiered Jewelry Box
WITH SLIDING TRAY

BY BILL PARRIE

Materials:
  Moulding:
    Larson-Juhl #643IG, lid and box
    Larson-Juhl #102CG, fillet trim for tray ledge
    Larson-Juhl #373IG, tray
  Matboard: Crescent Moorman #A7201

Box size: 20-1/2 x 17-3/4 x 7"

1) Lid is a simple frame with artwork installed under glass.
2) Measure outside edge of lid and cut moulding to fit, rabbet side down.
3) Create base, rabbet side down so outside of edge of bottom of box fits into the rabbet of the upper moulding.
4) Cut fillet 102CG to fit inside of box to form a ledge for the tray.
5) Cut moulding for tray 373IG to fit easily inside of lined box and sit on ledge—to slide back and forth to gain access to items below.
6) Cover all exposed surfaces with black moiré and add a black moiré board to bottom of box.
7) Cut out area to recess hinges.

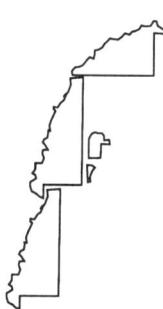

BURLWOOD BOX WITH BLACK KNOB

BY BILL PARRIE

Materials:
    Moulding:
        Larson-Juhl #603601
        Larson-Juhl Fillet #153IS
    Matboard: Crescent Moorman #A7201
    Black knob

1) Cut four triangles, 45 degree angle, with long flat side of triangle at rabbet of moulding. Join this square. This is the lid.
2) Cut 4 pieces of fillet to nestle in the "dip" in lid. Glue in place.
3) Attach knob to center of lid. Cover underside of lid with black moiré matboard.
4) Moulding for box base is used rabbet down, face out. Adjust size to fit the lid.
5) Line box with black moiré matboard.
6) Cut fillet to trim top edge of base.
7) Cover bottom of box with black moiré matboard.

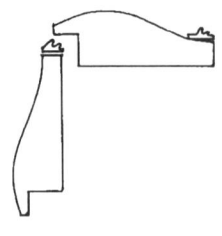
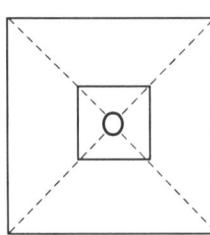

BUSINESS CARD HOLDER

BY BILL PARRIE

Materials:
    Moulding: Larson-Juhl #603601
            Larson-Juhl fillet #104601
    Matboard: Crescent Moorman #A7201

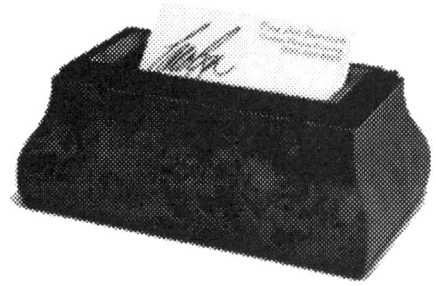

1) Use moulding rabbet down, face out. Rabbet of frame is bottom of box. The size of opening at top of box should be 3-3/4 x 1-1/2".
2) Fill rabbet of frame with a piece of black moiré matboard and foam center board.
3) Line interior of box with black moiré matboard.
4) Trim top edge of cardholder with fillet to finish the edge and conceal the edge of the matboard lining.
5) Cover bottom with black moiré matboard and felt pads or Bumpons®.

DESK ACCESSORIES
BY BOB MAYFIELD

Materials:
    Moulding:
        LaMarche #R7599
    Matboard: Crescent Moorman #7522
    Black linen
    3" core cardboard tube, 2" tall

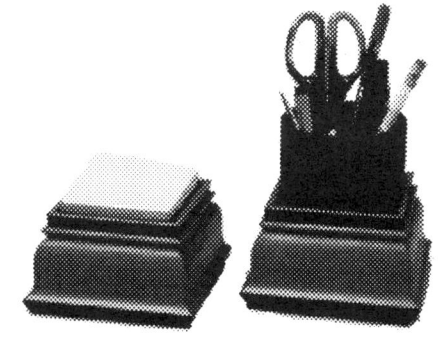

POST-IT® HOLDER
1) Cut box rabbet up face out, 3-1/4" rabbet measure.
2) Cut a layer of scrap board to fit rabbet. Cover with a piece of linen matboard. Glue into rabbet of box.
3) Cover bottom with linen matboard.

PENCIL CUP
1) Create the box rabbet up face out, 3-1/4" rabbet measure.
2) Cut a layer of scrap board to fit rabbet. Cut a piece of black linen board to match. Cut a 2-1/2" circle opening in each.
3) Glue boards into rabbet of box. Line circle opening with strip of linen.
4) Cover 3" core tube piece with black linen.
5) Set wrapped cylinder on top of box.
6) Cover bottom of box with black linen board.

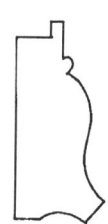

CHERRY BOX WITH BALL FEET
BY CAROLYN BIRCHENALL

With a creative eye and decorative embellishment, boxes can have any character from traditional to contemporary, from serious to playful. This delightful little box is a great example of expressive design.

Materials:
    Moulding:
        Piedmont #13-86-104, lid
        Piedmont #20-88-104, sides
    Matboard: Crescent Moorman #7552
    Wood beads

The top section is slightly larger than the bottom, allowing the top to fit over the bottom lip.

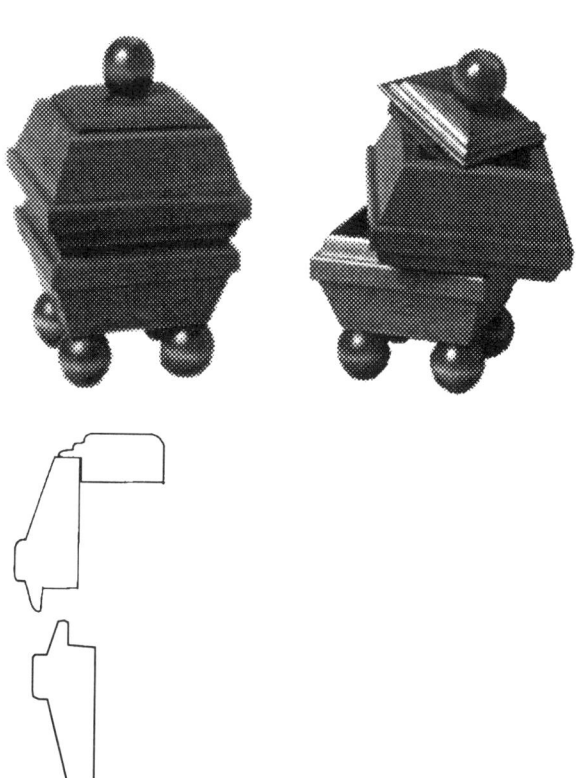

SILVER BOX

BY JENNIFER KOCSIS

This box is designed with the broadest edge of the moulding facing upward, creating a graceful combination of vertical and horizontal projection.

Materials:
Moulding:
      Larson-Juhl #300CS, lid
      Larson-Juhl #500CS, box base
Matboard: Crescent Moorman #7183

1) Cut base moulding rabbet up, face out, each piece measuring 6" outside.
2) Fill rabbet with foam center board and cover with linen matboard. This is the bottom of the box.
3) Line interior with matboard.
4) Cut lid pieces as a typical picture frame, each piece 4" outside. Save the four scrap triangles created while cutting lid.
5) Join lid. Join the scrap triangles into a small square. Glue the little square to the larger one to create a one piece lid, or leave loose to create a little "secret compartment".
6) Cover underside of lid with suede matboard. Attach to this another piece of same board slightly smaller than the opening of the lined box, so lid rests securely on box.

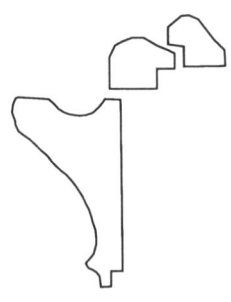

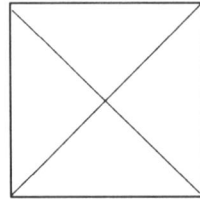

Scrap triangles can be joined to form a tiny top. This can be attached to the frame permanently or left as another compartment.

TISSUE BOX/RECEPTION BOX

BY BILL PARRIE

This elegant stacking of five layers of moulding begins with Larson-Juhl #435AB, cut and joined as a typical frame with a rabbet measurement of 1-1/2" x 3-3/4". The next three layers are cut to fit each previous layer.

Mouldings:
Larson-Juhl #435AB, top
Larson-Juhl #403IG
Larson-Juhl #153IG
Larson-Juhl #403IG
Larson-Juhl #683IG, bottom

To make a holder for square boxes of tissue, cover the bottom with a suede mat, leaving a 5x5" opening. A fillet could be used to edge the opening of the box.

To make a wedding reception box to hold cards and cash gifts, increase the opening size in the top layer and make a removable fabric-covered matboard bottom.

ETCHED MIRROR BOX

BY BILL PARRIE

Materials
Moulding:
Larson-Juhl #X2343, lid
Larson-Juhl #X2362, base
Matboard: Crescent Moorman #7195
Etched mirror

1) Build lid frame to hold a 4 x 6" etched mirror.
2) Fit mirror in frame (see page 9) and cover back of lid with suede matboard.
3) Build base to fit lid. Use moulding rabbet up, face out. Lid will rest on the rabbet of this frame.
4) Line base with suede matboard. Cover bottom of box with same color board. Nail or glue board in place.

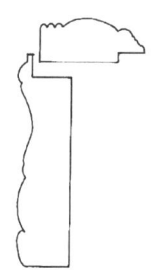

WALL SHELF WITH INSET TOP

BY CAROLYN BIRCHENALL

Make small display shelves or a full-sized mantel to hang over a fireplace. Simply determine the width and depth needed, then design the height according to the character and massiveness you want. Top surfaces can be wood, mirror, marble, faux-finished or fabric-covered matboard.

Materials:
Moulding:
   Larson-Juhl #643G
   1 x 2" lumber or strainer length
Scrap matboard
Mirror
Hanging hardware

1) Determine desired length and depth of shelf and cut the front and side moulding pieces rabbet down, face out. The front rail will have a 45 degree angle at both ends. The side rails need a 45 degree angle at the outer edge, and a straight cut at the end that will touch the wall. Join the three pieces.
2) Cut a piece of lumber or strainer to fit inside the length of the shelf. Glue and nail this support strip inside back of shelf.
3) Cut a piece of matboard to fit top of shelf. This will rest in the rabbet of the moulding. Cut mirror to same size.
4) Cover back of shelf.
5) Attach hanging hardware to the strainer strip.

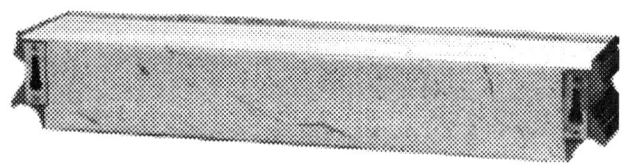

Keyhole hangers have been recessed into the two ends of the shelf. The shelf will hang very tight to the wall using these types of hangers.

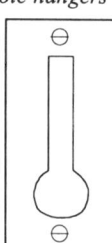

Keyhole hangers

CIGAR OR TOBACCO HUMIDOR

BY BILL PARRIE

Fine cigars and tobacco require specialized storage. A cigar will last indefinitely, with no loss of quality or flavor, if kept at 70 dcgrccs Fahrenheit and 70% humidity. The temperature is not difficult to achieve, since 70 degrees is the approximate comfortable room temperature in any house with central heating and air conditioning. The consistent high moisture is more difficult to maintain, which is why a humidor is an essential accessory for any afficionado of the smoking arts. These cedar-lined containers, equipped with the means to maintain and measure humidity levels, create an optimum environment for tobacco storage.

Materials:

Moulding:
Larson-Juhl #369712, center of lid
Larson-Juhl #619723, lid and box base
Larson-Juhl #603601, lid
Larson-Juhl #X2133, fillet trim

Matboard as bottom cover: Crescent Moorman #A7201
Quadrant hinges (one pair)
Humidity regulator (attaches to inside of lid)
1/8" Spanish cedar sheets

1) Construct the lid as a normal frame, but without an opening window—the mouldings will touch each other at the rabbet side. Cut two pieces of #369712, approximately 9-1/2" long, Lay these pieces rabbet-to-rabbet. Cut triangular end pieces to fit each end, forming a rectangle.

2) Cut and join #619723 to fit around the center rectangle. Cut and join #603601 to fit around #619723. Attach the three frames together.

3) Cut and join #619723, cut rabbet down, face out. Outer edge of this layer should be same size as outer edge of humidor lid.

4) Cut and join #369712, cut rabbet down, face out to fit in the rabbet of the previous frame.

5) Cut and join #603601, cut rabbet down, face out to fit in the rabbet of the previous frame.

6) Attach the three base layers together using glue and nails.

7) A fillet bottom edge will create a "foot" styling and finish the project handsomely.

8) Use 1/8" Spanish cedar to line the box and lid. Cut carefully to fit. Do not use nails or glue because the cedar must be able to absorb and release moisture.

9) To make two levels, add a short piece of cedar to the lower section of the box. This will support the tray. All cedar pieces must be loose, the cut and fit is important. Glue may be used to build the tray. Notice the strips of cedar used for the tray are spaced and cut diagonally to allow air circulation and to keep the cigars from falling through the slats.

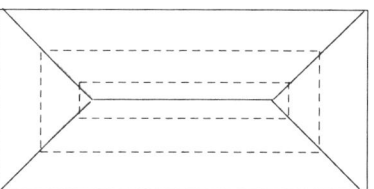

Two mouldings "connect" to form the lid.

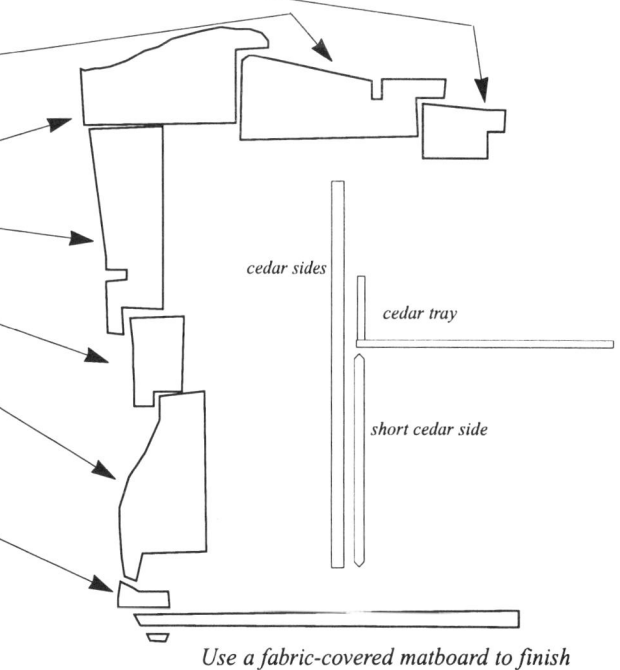

cedar sides

cedar tray

short cedar side

Use a fabric-covered matboard to finish the bottom of the box.

Octagons

Octagon are cut at 67.5 degrees. This may be obvious when the box is evenly spaced as the two on this page are, however, the same angle is used for the two projects on the next page.

Gold Octagon with Brass Knob

BY BILL PARRIE

Materials:

    Moulding:

        Larson-Juhl #6831G, lid

        Larson-Juhl #4031G, upper base

        Larson-Juhl #6431G, base

1) Cut 8 triangles from 6813G rabbet out, 2" at the rabbet. Join to form octagonal lid.
2) Build upper base from Larson-Juhl #403IG, cut as an ordinary octagon picture frame, to fit lid.
3) Build lower layer from Larson-Juhl #643IG, cut rabbet up, face out to fit upper base.
4) Line all exposed interior surfaces with black silk matboard. Attach upper base to lower base. Fill bottom with a piece of foam center board sandwiched between two pieces of silk matboard, one piece facing outward, the other facing inward.

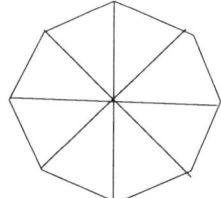

White Marble Octagon Box

BY BILL AND BETTY HURSEY

This elegant box has a formal, opulent look. The crystal knob adds the crowning touch.

Materials:

    Moulding:

        Williamson #58-818-0-831

    Fabric-covered matboard for lining

    Crystal cabinet knob

1) Mouldings are cut as normal frames but using 67.5 degree cuts for the octagon. Start by making the lid. Then fit each layer to the one above.

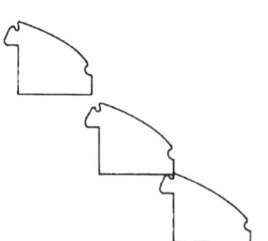

Octagon Shelf and Matching Mirror

By Bill Parrie
Moulding:
  Larson-Juhl #683IG, mirror and shelf base

A wall shelf with angled corners is essentially half of an octagon frame. The angled pieces are cut at 67.5 degrees, and the two ends that will touch the wall have straight cuts.

The mirror is a basic octagon frame.

The shelf surface is a faux marble finished piece of wood. Tops may extend over the edge of the shelf or fit into the rabbet.

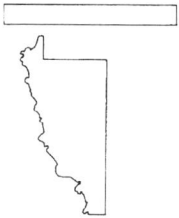

Long Octagon Box

By Bill and Betty Hursey
Materials
  Moulding:
    Zinsel #080061 GP, lid
    Zinsel #080078 GP, base
  Hardware for handle
  Fabric-covered matboard to line the box

This octagon is just a simple moulding used rabbet up face out for the sides of the box, with coordinating moulding used for the lid.

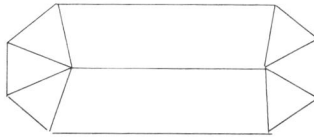

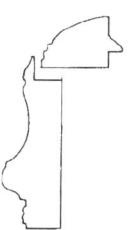

Both the lid and box use the same 67.5 degree cuts. The measurement of the long side of the box and lid must match. Make the lid first, then cut the base to fit.

CURIO CABINET

BY BILL PARRIE

Design a cabinet to display a particular collection, serve as a functional but attractive storage unit, or use as a retail merchandise case. Since the cabinet and all of the shelves can be made in any size desired, the items contained can fit comfortably in their space.

Materials:

Mouldings:

Larson-Juhl #317601, door and shelves
Larson-Juhl #104601, fillet trim inside door
Larson-Juhl #603601, box

Matboard: Crescent Moorman #67114
Glazier's points to hold in glass
Glass for door
Hanging hardware

Overall cabinet size is 14 x 24" x 1-1/2" deep

1) Build door first. Cut and join a regular 45 degree angle frame using #317601. Fit glass into frame rabbet. Trim inside of door with fillet #104601. Line inside edge of door with fabric matboard.

2) Using the door size as your measurement, join #603601 rabbet down, face out to make the box. Attach a decorative fillet border flush with inside front edge of box.

3) Line sides of box with a fabric-covered matboard.

4) Make three shelves using #317601. Join front pieces rabbet up, face out, with a miter on both ends. Then cut the side pieces, with a straight cut at one end and a miter at the other. Join these three-side-shelves. Space evenly inside box and attach to sides with nails. Countersink and fill nail holes. If the underside of the moulding is unfinished, paint or stain it to coordinate with the fabric covering.

5) Install a piece of fabric-covered matboard, along with a supporting layer of foam center board, into the back side of the box. The rabbet will hold both boards. Glue and nail in place.

6) Hinge door to box.

7) Attach hanging hardware to back of box, routing out hinge area for a recessed fit.

Inside of cabinet box

On the back side of cabinet, the rabbet will accommodate a sheet of foam center board and a sheet of matboard to serve as a finished back.

top view of shelf

Fabric-covered matboard will fit into rabbet to create the shelf. Add a piece of foam center board to fill the rabbet.

SCONCES

BY CAROLYN BIRCHENALL

Beautiful wall sconces can be made by layering mouldings vertically, beginning at the bottom. Make a rounded style by cutting all the pieces in a layer to equal size, or create a wider display surface by elongating the center front piece of each layer. If making a pair, cut both at once.

Materials:

Mouldings:
Decor #6464, two bottom layers
Victor #11537, middle layer
Victor #205, top layer
Matboard: Crescent vinyl moiré #1902
Glue and Nails
Bracing strips (to support drying layers)
Hanging hardware (two for each sconce)
Wooden ball (one for bottom of each sconce)

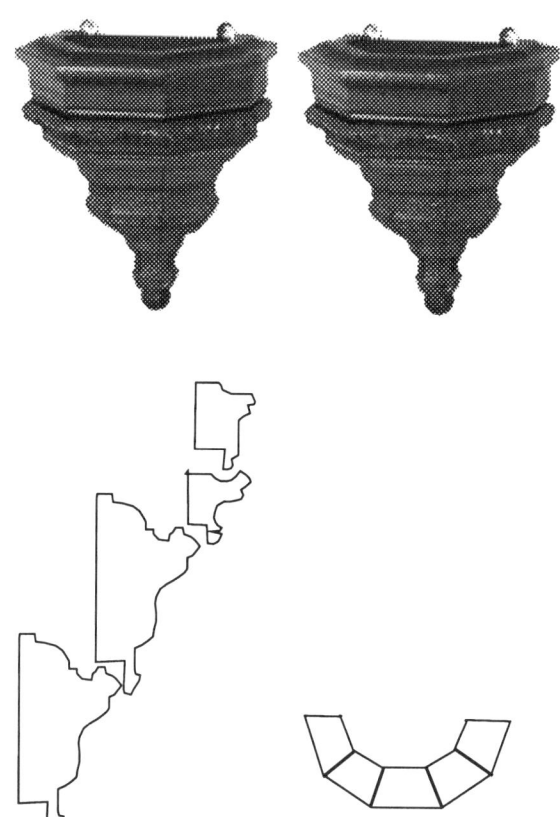

1) Cut bottom layer first, to establish size. The goal is to create a half-circle that will rest flat against the wall, so begin with two pieces cut at a 45 degree angle, to create flat-backed end pieces for this layer. Cut the other end of these moulding pieces, and all the pieces in between them, at 67.5 degree angles. This is a cut-to-fit project, so shave and adjust as necessary to make the moulding pieces meet comfortably.

2) Glue bottom layer pieces together. This bottom layer will require some creative joining techniques, as the small, angled pieces must be held in place and allowed to set one by one. Devise a clamping system, or it may be most practical to simply hold the glued sections by hand, adding a new piece as soon as the glue firms up on the last one.

3) Next layer—decide where this layer will rest on lower layer. Join moulding, rabbet down, two pieces with flat back and 67.5 degree angle on the rest of the pieces. Join the layer into a half-round, then attach with glue to the bottom layer.

4) Continue for next three layers. With larger layers, glue together using the Strap Clamp* to secure. Brace the interior with pieces of strainer or other wood. This support will be necessary to hold the hanging hardware.

5) Attach hanging hardware to back of sconce. Add a bead, ball, or other ornament to bottom of the sconce if desired.

6) Line top surface with matboard to create a shelf. Cover back of sconce with matboard.